I'M GOOD AT
LANGUAGES
WHAT JOB CAN I GET?

Richard Spilsbury

WAYLAND

Published in 2014 by Wayland
Copyright © Wayland 2014

Wayland
338 Euston Road
London NW1 3BH

Wayland Australia
Level 17/207
Kent Street
Sydney, NSW 2000

Produced for Wayland by
White-Thomson Publishing Ltd
www.wtpub.co.uk
+44 (0)843 2087 460

Commissioning editor: Victoria Brooker
Project editor: Kelly Davis
Designer: Tim Mayer
Picture research: Richard Spilsbury
Proofreader and indexer: Lucy Ross

Dewey categorisation: 418'.0023-dc23

ISBN-13: 9780750284202

First published in 2013 by Wayland

Printed in China

10 9 8 7 6 5 4 3 2 1

Wayland is a division of Hachette
Children's Books, an Hachette UK company.
www.hachette.co.uk

Picture credits

1, Dreamstime/Ggprophoto; 3, Shutterstock/ Andresr; 4, Dreamstime/Americanspirit; 5, Dreamstime/Alptraum; 6, Dreamstime/ Amaranta; 7, Shutterstock/Dmitrijs Dmitrijevs; 8, Dreamstime/Thanatonautii; 9, Dreamstime/Muxiang; 10, Dreamstime/ Monkeybusinessimages; 11, Dreamstime/ Ggprophoto; 12, Dreamstime/Dteurope; 13, Dreamstime/Christiankieffer; 14, Dreamstime/ Serkovfoto; 15, Dreamstime/Syaochka; 16, Dreamstime/Nito100; 17, Dreamstime/ Rcaucino; 18, Dreamstime/Lordface; 19, Dreamstime/Aniram; 20, Shutterstock/withGod; 21, Shutterstock/Andresr; 22 Dreamstime/ Kojoku; 23, Dreamstime/Snyderdf; 24, Dreamstime/Taolmor; 25, Shutterstock/Netfalls – Remy Musser; 26, Dreamstime/Yuri_arcurs; 27, Dreamstime/Hupeng; 28, Dreamstime/ Paulprescott; 29, Dreamstime/Americanspirit; cover (top left),Dreamstime/Muxiang; cover (top right), Shutterstock/Dmitrijs Dmitrijevs; cover (bottom), Shutterstock/Syaheir Azizan.

CONTENTS

The world of languages   4

Translator   6

Interpreter   8

Language teacher   10

Bilingual secretary   12

Diplomatic service officer   14

Overseas resort representative   16

European Union official   18

Flight attendant   20

Aid worker   22

Immigration officer   24

Marketing campaign manager   26

Foreign correspondent   28

Glossary   30

Further information   31

Index   32

The world of languages

Language is essential to every aspect of our everyday lives. We use words to tell other people what we feel and what we want, and to gain information. Foreign language skills can open up the world to us, making travel easier and providing exciting work opportunities.

↑ There are around 6000 languages in the world and only 6 per cent of the global population speaks English. Knowledge of foreign languages is a valuable asset in our multicultural society.

The importance of languages

Being able to communicate with people from different cultures and countries in their own language helps us to form bonds and share experiences. Language skills also allow us to work in team with people of other nationalities, and understand differences an similarities. Knowing how to speak a foreign language can ease tensions between individuals and groups (such as opposing side in a war), and improve international relations.

Many businesses need workers with language skills. One in five exporting companies say that language and cultural barriers lose them business.

Languages in the workplace

Speaking other languages can make buying and selling goods or services, and dealing with business partners, much easier. This is true when communicating with companies or organisations in the 27 countries of the European Union (EU), to which the UK belongs. It is also vital in the markets of increasingly important and wealthy countries such as China, India, Russia and Brazil. Many employers see language skills as an asset, and an ability to speak and understand foreign languages can help you find your ideal job in a range of industries, from banking to tourism.

PROFESSIONAL VIEWPOINT

'If I'm selling to you, I speak your language. If I'm buying, dann müssen Sie Deutsch sprechen!' [meaning: 'If I'm buying, you should speak German (my language)']
Willy Brandt, former German chancellor

Special skills

Being good at languages means you can rapidly learn the grammar, sounds and pronunciation of other languages. You will be able to identify the grammatical patterns and structure of your chosen languages, and spot differences from (and similarities to) your own. This requires initiative and analytical and organisational skills, and also good written and verbal communication skills. These qualities are useful in specific language careers and also more generally in other jobs. Read on to find out about some of the career paths you could follow.

Translator

Are you good at quickly converting written text from one language to another? If so, then you might like to become a translator. Professional translators usually translate into their own language so they can more easily retain both the content and the meaning of the original version.

− Job description −

Translators:

- read material and rewrite it in one or several other languages
- use specialist dictionaries and reference books to find appropriate words and phrases
- proofread and edit final translated versions
- negotiate and work to agreed deadlines and prices for jobs.

↓ At international book fairs, publishers make deals with authors to sell their works in different countries. They employ skilled translators to convert the text.

What skills do I need?

Translators usually have a degree in two languages and they are often fluent in more. Some study translation or business with languages. To be a good translator, you also need a knowledge of the cultures of the languages you speak, which is often gained through living abroad. The languages most in demand include not only European ones (such as French, German and Spanish) but also, increasingly, Chinese, Arabic and Russian. Attention to detail, excellent proofreading skills, and the ability to write well in your own language and work quickly to meet deadlines are also key skills for translators.

↑ Some translators create audio guides to help tourists of different nationalities enjoy visiting famous sites and attractions.

Different types of translator

Many translators work on particular kinds of text. For example, some specialise in technical texts (such as car manuals or furniture assembly instructions), while others work on legal documents. Some translate original works of fiction and poetry for publishers. Others translate information for websites and subtitles for DVDs and video games. Most translators work as freelancers from home, either for translation agencies or directly for clients, although a number of organisations employ in-house translators.

PROFESSIONAL VIEWPOINT

'You need an in-depth knowledge of your working languages and of the cultures to which they belong, excellent written skills and a capacity to research and learn very quickly, as you might not be a specialist in all the areas covered by the documents you'll be asked to translate.'
Céline Graciet, French-to-English translator

Interpreter

Interpreters use their language skills to translate spoken words in an instant. Their job is to provide live communication between people who speak different languages, such as police officers and suspects, or politicians from different countries at meetings or conferences.

↓

Interpreters play a valuable role in conflict zones, where their work can aid communication between opposing sides or allies who speak different languages.

Job description

Interpreters:
- listen carefully to a speaker's words
- immediately translate the ideas expressed from that language into another
- build up a knowledge of key vocabulary in their specialist area, such as sport or the environment
- carry out research before translating for meetings, lectures or speeches on specific topics
- may need to keep what they have heard confidential – for instance, when working for governments, companies or heads of state.

Interpreting requires a lot of concentration. You may have to attend many meetings and translate long or complicated speeches.

What skills do I need?

Interpreters should be confident about public speaking, and have a good memory and powers of concentration as well as the ability to stay calm under pressure. You should be quick-thinking, be exact in your use of grammar and have complete mastery of another language, including unusual phrases, slang and even jokes! Most interpreters have a language degree, experience of living and working in a place where the foreign language is used, and often a postgraduate diploma or master's degree in interpreting techniques.

Different types of interpreter

There are two kinds of interpreter – simultaneous and consecutive. Simultaneous interpreters work in a soundproof booth, translating instantaneously. For example, at a large meeting they might interpret what a speaker says for people who don't speak the same language. Consecutive interpreters give an accurate account of what a speaker has said after they have spoken. These interpreters' summaries may be used by foreign journalists – for instance, at a sports star's press conference. Interpreters need to be on the spot for their work, so the job can involve a lot of travel.

Language teacher

If you enjoy speaking a foreign language and would love to be able to pass on your knowledge, this could be the job for you. Language teachers help their students to converse, read, write and study in a language other than their native one.

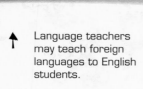

↑ Language teachers may teach foreign languages to English students.

Job description

Language teachers:
• plan, prepare and deliver lessons that engage students and help them develop language skills
• set comprehension tests and exercises
• mark oral and written work and give feedback on it
• prepare students for exams
• devise materials, including audio and visual resources, for their classes
• manage classes of students and attendance records.

Different types of language teacher

Many language teachers specialise in teaching one or several languages to groups of different ages or abilities. They may focus on students at secondary school, college or university, or adults learning at their workplace or in evening classes. Other teachers work in language schools, either in the UK or abroad, teaching English as a foreign language (EFL). Some language teachers are freelancers who offer private tuition to people who want to improve their language skills.

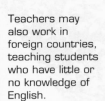

Teachers may also work in foreign countries, teaching students who have little or no knowledge of English.

What skills do I need?

It goes without saying that you will have an interest in language and culture, and very good communication skills. But you will also require patience – it can take longer for some students to learn languages – and a willingness to find the most effective ways to teach different groups. You will also need to be well organised and have the confidence and authority to control a class. Language teachers are either native speakers of the language they are teaching or they have a university degree in it, as well as a recognised teaching qualification such as a PGCE.

Bilingual secretary

Would you like to combine your foreign language skills with an office role? If so, a bilingual secretary's job might be ideal for you. Bilingual secretaries, or multilingual personal assistants (PAs), do what any secretary does, but in two languages!

Bilingual secretaries often work in international travel or law firms, international organisations such as the United Nations, or companies involved in importing and exporting goods. Their administrative duties may include translating, word-processing and archiving documents using one or more foreign languages. They also email and speak to foreign contacts, work on company multilingual websites, act as interpreters at meetings or for telephone calls, and organise meetings and hospitality for visitors.

What skills do I need?

As for most secretarial roles, you should have good IT, organisational and presentational skills. Some bilingual secretaries have a degree in languages or a combined languages and business studies qualification, although this is not essential. Generally the minimum requirement is at least an A-level or equivalent in your second language, unless it is your native tongue or you became fluent by living abroad.

← A bilingual secretary must be able to type, take shorthand and communicate in a foreign language.

Bilingual secretaries often handle arrangements (including hotel bookings and travel itineraries) when international clients visit a company. They may also act as interpreters during the visit.

Job description

Bilingual secretaries:

- answer telephone calls and take messages in a foreign language
- use digital recorders to record material for translation
- translate documents and letters between two languages, and produce letters, emails and reports
- organise meetings and keep track of appointments
- act as interpreters or translators when required
- book transport and accommodation for overseas visits or for international visitors
- update computer databases.

Diplomatic service officer

If you are interested in international affairs, you might like to become a diplomatic service officer. Your job will be to promote your country's interests overseas and protect your citizens when they go abroad. As a diplomat, you will mainly work for the Foreign and Commonwealth Office (FCO) and will often be stationed in other countries.

PROFESSIONAL VIEWPOINT

'One of the biggest challenges is also one of the greatest perks and that is living overseas. We move to a new country every few years. While that is exciting, I spend a lot of my life with my possessions in boxes, learning the quirks of a new country, and meeting new co-workers.'

Shawn Cobb, diplomat

The FCO has embassies and other official premises (where diplomatic service officers work) in more th 170 countries, including this one in Moscow, Russ

What skills do I need?

You will be good at communicating with a wide range of people from different cultural backgrounds. You will also be skilled at solving problems rapidly, in the interests of your own country, but also taking into account the needs of local people. To join the FCO, you must meet a variety of nationality and residency requirements, and pass several tests. Most applicants have a degree (in any subject) and some experience of travelling or living in foreign countries.

Different types of diplomatic service officer

Political officers monitor political and economic developments in a country. They report back to the British government, advise on foreign policy, and represent Britain's interests to that country's government and media. Commercial officers help British companies to trade in a country, and foreign companies to trade in Britain. Consular officers assist British citizens in a country – for example, by issuing travel safety advice – and process visa applications from local people wishing to visit Britain.

↑ Diplomatic service officers should be willing to work anywhere in the world. Many move to a number of different countries with their families during their careers.

Job description

Diplomatic service officers:
- deal with correspondence, accounts and other administrative tasks
- commission, draft and proofread written reports
- may run an office, recruit and organise staff
- chair meetings and prepare documents beforehand
- assist British citizens and businesses abroad
- liaise with high commissions and embassies representing governments
- inform the media about British policies.

Overseas resort representative

Are you good at organising group activities, putting people at their ease and solving problems? Do you like the idea of working in travel and tourism? If so, you might like to be a resort representative. Representatives (known as reps) look after holidaymakers abroad, and liaise with local people to make sure that visitors enjoy their trip.

Coastal resort reps may have to organise anything from renting beach umbrellas to finding restaurants where people with food allergies can eat safely.

Job description

Overseas resort representatives:
• meet holidaymakers at airports or sea ports and accompany them to their accommodation
• give information about resort facilities and local attractions and rules or customs
• arrange, and sometimes accompany guests on, excursions, sightseeing trips and leisure activities
• are available to give advice and deal with problems like lost passports or money, illness or difficulties with accommodation
• keep records, and write reports about complaints and incidents such as illness.

What skills do I need?

Reps need to be outgoing, good listeners, and enjoy meeting and organising groups of people. You will be interested in travel, other cultures and the impact of tourism. It helps to be fluent in one or more foreign languages. Many resort employers ask for GCSE passes and then offer on-the-job training. However, you could gain some of the skills and knowledge you need by taking a course such as a BTEC or a degree in tourism.

A winter holiday resort rep may have to arrange ski excursions for holidaymakers.

PROFESSIONAL VIEWPOINT

'You've got to remember that, in some ways, you're the public face of the resort so you've constantly got to project a positive image regardless of the circumstances. It's also important to be in control of the situation whatever eventualities may arise.'

Becky Ellinson, resort representative

Different types of overseas resort representative

A rep's work varies according to the resort they work in. These can range from winter sports centres to summer beach resorts, and from cruise ships to desert cities. Reps have many general duties, such as meeting and greeting visitors, inspecting accommodation, organising excursions and dealing with problems (for example, loss or theft of items and rowdy behaviour). They also have duties that are specific to their resort, such as arranging ski hire or scuba diving.

European Union official

The European Union (EU) is an organisation representing the economic and political interests of over 500 million people in most European countries. If you are interested in European current affairs, you might like to become an official who helps formulate and implement the policies of the EU.

PROFESSIONAL VIEWPOINT

'I've had the chance to see how big political decisions are taken and have witnessed extraordinary events, but it's working every day with people from 27 countries that makes this job endlessly varied – it opens your eyes to a much wider range of perspectives than you encounter at home.'

Ralph Pines, EU official

↓ Most EU officials regularly work in or visit the central offices of the organisation in Brussels, Belgium.

European Union officials:

- help draft new laws in areas such as trade, environment, science and technology, and transport
- take part in negotiations with non-EU countries
- put new policies into practice
- attend meetings and conferences
- research topics and prepare reports
- answer questions from members of the European Parliament
- manage staff and finances.

Many EU officials have to make speeches, present reports and answer questions about issues affecting Europe.

Different types of European Union official

EU officials work in various departments. The largest, the European Commission, is responsible for organising common policies for the member countries and running the EU. Some officials deal with agriculture or fisheries, and others with giving aid to non-EU countries. Officials in the Court of Justice and the European Parliament help make new laws and check that countries obey EU laws. Many officials work in several different departments during their careers.

What skills do I need?

To be good at this job, you will have excellent spoken and written communication skills. You should also be able to use your initiative and be a logical thinker. To work for an EU institution, you must be a citizen of an EU member state, be able to speak at least a second EU language, and will usually have a degree in a subject such as politics, European history or modern languages. Graduates can gain useful work experience through the European Commission Traineeship Scheme and many start out as administrators, helping more senior officials.

Flight attendant

If you like meeting different people and enjoy travelling the world, this career could be ideal for you. Flight attendants (also known as air cabin crew members or stewards) help ensure that airline passengers have a comfortable, safe and pleasant flight.

↑ Flight attendants are responsible for preparing and delivering food and drinks to passengers.

Job description

Flight attendants:
- check supplies and emergency equipment before take-off
- greet passengers and direct them to their seats
- demonstrate emergency procedures
- serve and sell food, drinks and goods
- make sure passengers are comfortable and deal with any requests
- make announcements on behalf of the pilot
- ensure that everyone leaves the plane safely, with all their hand luggage
- write flight reports, including any unusual incidents
- reassure passengers in the event of an emergency, and make sure they follow safety procedures.

Flight attendants work shifts, which can include weekends, nights and public holidays. The amount of time they spend away from home varies, depending on whether the flights are national or international. Most flight attendants are employed by large commercial airlines, but some work on private jets. Some of the work can be physically demanding, such as taking refreshments to passengers, helping to load luggage into lockers and assisting people on and off planes. Between flights, attendants often have opportunities to explore the destinations they have flown to.

→ Attendants check that passengers are safely belted into their seats before take-off and landing.

What skills do I need?

People skills are important in this job, as you will have to deal with a wide variety of passengers. You will also be expected to dress smartly and speak and listen well. You will need at least four GCSEs (including English and maths), and it is especially important to speak one or more foreign languages if you plan to work for an airline based in a non-English speaking country. Most airlines will expect you to complete courses on first aid, safety procedures and customer service.

Aid worker

When you see headlines about people being affected by volcanoes, earthquakes or other natural disasters, or displaced by war, do you wish you could do something to help? Aid workers manage and develop emergency response programmes worldwide, giving humanitarian assistance that saves lives, reduces suffering and improves welfare.

↑ Aid workers distribute food to people in need.

Job description

Aid workers:
- assess what help is needed in emergency situations
- write reports and proposals for intervention
- work with local staff and other emergency departments
- monitor the effectiveness of activities and liaise with UN workers and government officials
- follow up-to-date security and safety procedures
- provide information for donors, local authorities and aid organisations about what funds are required for different purposes
- manage budgets and produce funding proposals.

← Aid workers interview locals affected by an earthquake in Haiti. Their job is to assess the particular type of assistance people require.

Many aid workers operate in places where disasters have struck, distributing aid, which ranges from emergency food and medical supplies to materials for building shelters. Some work in offices in the UK, encouraging the public to make donations to pay for the aid. Many different charities, international non-governmental organisations (NGOs), private trusts or foundations and voluntary not-for-profit groups are involved in providing aid. Some of them supply specialised aid (such as treatment to prevent blindness, carried out by Sightsavers), while others (like Save the Children) offer more general humanitarian aid.

What skills do I need?

You should have enthusiasm, commitment and good communication skills in both English and local languages. Specialist knowledge is important, and a degree in languages, medicine, engineering or social sciences can be especially useful. Many aid workers start out by gaining experience as volunteers, and most major aid agencies provide details about how to get voluntary internships on their websites.

Immigration officer

Immigration officers monitor the people who enter and leave their country at borders. This is an important job because these officers can identify and control the movement of illegal immigrants. Some immigrants may need assistance in escaping danger in their own country, whereas others may be criminals or could be arriving to work illegally.

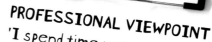

PROFESSIONAL VIEWPOINT

'I spend time researching the ways in which people try to gain illegal entry into the UK, and use this intelligence to help strengthen our border controls. On the surveillance side, I monitor flights arriving at Heathrow. Our aim is to stop passengers who don't have permission from entering the UK.'

John, immigration officer

Some immigration officers work at international entry points to the UK, such as Dover port or Heathrow airport. They check the landing cards and passports of non-British and non-European passengers, to see if they meet the criteria for entry into the country. Officers also investigate foreign nationals who are already in the country (for example, working in businesses), and gather intelligence to confirm whether or not they are illegal immigrants. When necessary, immigration officers use legal powers to remove illegal entrants from the country.

← Part of an immigration officer's job is to recognise the fake passports that people sometimes use to gain illegal entry into a country.

What skills do I need?

Immigration officers have to be confident, responsible and able to work under pressure. They must also be firm when following immigration laws, even when it is distressing to refuse vulnerable people entry into the country. They need clear spoken and written communication skills and good powers of observation. Many applicants will be educated to A-level standard or higher and have some language skills. Previous experience of working face-to-face with the public would be helpful.

← Some immigration officers work at border control points, monitoring the movement of people entering a country.

Job description

Immigration officers:

- examine passports and look out for counterfeit documents
- interview passengers to find out information about them
- arrange for people who have been refused entry to be detained or go back to their point of departure
- organise surveillance of suspected illegal immigrants
- visit and interview people who are suspected of having no right to remain in the UK
- write and present case study reports and statistics.

Marketing campaign managers

To be globally successful, companies need to encourage different groups of customers around the world to buy their products or services. International marketing campaign managers identify who and where potential purchasers are. They also work with teams of people to design and manage campaigns, using a range of promotional techniques to attract interest and sales.

↓

Marketing campaign managers use their communication skills to collaborate with clients and develop strong campaign ideas.

Job description

Marketing campaign managers:

- liaise with clients and contractors about key selling points for products and services
- develop marketing content
- organise media coverage, from press adverts to online promotion
- schedule and attend conferences, trade shows and other events
- check translations of marketing material, working with language experts when necessary
- advise on whether campaigns can be translated directly or need to be adapted for different markets and cultures
- produce sales reports that measure the success of marketing initiatives.

arketing campaign managers work with creative agencies to
roduce effective adverts in other languages for foreign markets.
hey buy advertising spaces in magazines, on billboards and TV
obally. They also develop website content and use social networks
spread the word about their products. Marketing managers may
nprove the success of these campaigns by communicating with
urnalists, clients, distributors and suppliers in their own languages.

Marketing campaigns may include creating
stands and material for display at international
trade fairs to generate interest in products.

PROFESSIONAL VIEWPOINT

'One day I might be overseeing a pitch to the marketing director visiting my office, and the next working through a celebrity product endorsement deal for another client in another country. Speaking the language really helps.'
Jack Mikkelson, marketing campaign manager

What skills do I need?

To be an effective international marketing campaign manager, you
should be creative and able to communicate ideas well in different
languages. Most marketing campaign managers have a degree
in languages or marketing, or they have business and marketing
experience. If you are studying business at school or college, why
not start a portfolio of ideas for campaigns that could help sell
products in different countries? You can then show your portfolio
to potential employers.

Foreign correspondent

Imagine there is breaking news in a foreign country – such as the election of a president or the outbreak of war – that is of interest to the rest of the world. Foreign correspondents are journalists who work overseas, seeking stories and creating news reports for publication or broadcast in their home countries' media.

→ Foreign correspondents live in other countries so they are ready to report on events as soon as they happen there.

Different types of foreign correspondent

Some foreign correspondents work for particular newspapers or television channels. Others are employed by news agencies such as Reuters, or they are freelance journalists who sell stories to a variety of different media. Foreign correspondents working for large news organisations usually specialise in particular regions, industries, or other areas such as energy or religion. Foreign correspondents may present news stories for TV and radio themselves, or help research and write reports that are presented by others.

Job description

Foreign correspondents:
- usually live in another country and learn about the local customs and culture
- gather information about changes in the country, and travel to key locations
- record facts accurately by observing events as they happen
- research public records and interview people affected by particular incidents
- communicate information clearly in an article for a newspaper or magazine or for a radio or television news broadcast.

Foreign correspondents often produce special human interest reports – for example, on the living conditions experienced by local people long after a natural disaster has occurred.

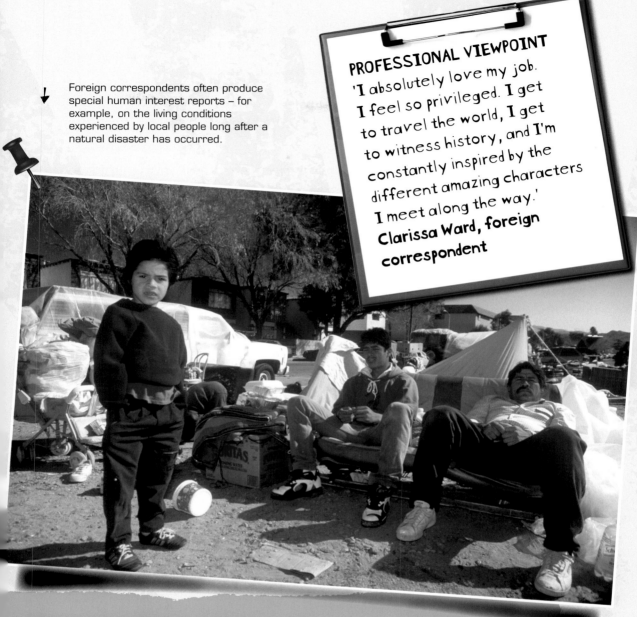

What skills do I need?

Foreign correspondents must be inquisitive and interested in world events. They need the drive and initiative to develop contacts and sources and conduct investigative research in a foreign country. It can take a lot of hard work to become established as a foreign correspondent. As well as holding a relevant undergraduate degree, such as politics, economics, journalism or history, fluency in at least two languages is beneficial, as is extensive journalistic experience and often a post-graduate qualification.

Glossary

aid emergency assistance (including food and shelter), following an event such as war, natural disaster or extreme weather

allies countries that co-operate with others, often for military reasons

analytical involving the use of reasoning and basic principles to solve problems

brainstorm group discussion to come up with spontaneous ideas

campaign (in advertising or marketing) a planned set of activities to raise awareness of a product or service

counterfeit fake and usually poorer copy of an original item; often called a forgery or imitation

criteria requirements

culture characteristics of a group of people, such as language, music, costume and religion

current affairs day-to-day political or social events that affect our lives

detain keep waiting or deny freedom of movement

displace force people or objects from their usual location or home; for example, villagers in a war zone may be displaced elsewhere to remain safe

European Union (EU) group of 27 countries in Europe whose governments work together to make laws in common

excursion short, organised outing taken for pleasure, such as a sightseeing or theatre trip

export sell goods to another country

fluent able to speak, read and write fast and accurately

freelancer someone who works independently on paid jobs for different employers

funding money provided for a particular purpose, such as building a new school

grammar rules by which sentences are constructed

humanitarian involving saving lives, reducing suffering and protecting human dignity

immigrant someone coming into a country from abroad, to make their home there

import buy goods from another country

in-house within a company or organisation, rather than outside it

international relations relationships between different countries worldwide

internship working for an employer to learn skills needed for a job

liaise talk to or communicate with people in order to work together

marketing business of finding out what people want to buy and how to sell things to them

multicultural made up of several different cultures

multilingual able to speak and write several languages

natural disaster earthquake, volcano, hurricane, tornado, or other natural event that negatively affects living things

portfolio collection of a person's creative work demonstrating their abilities

pronunciation the way a word is spoken

proofread to examine a copy or proof to find errors and mark corrections

social network web-based service (such as Facebook) that allows communication between people

surveillance observation by the authorities (such as the police or security services)

United Nations (UN) international organisation representing all the countries in the world

word-processing using a computer to create, edit and print documents

Further information

There are many specific courses, apprenticeships and jobs using language skills, so where do you go to find out more? It is really useful to meet up with careers advisers at school or college and to attend careers fairs to see the range of opportunities. Remember that public libraries and newspapers are other important sources of information. The earlier you check out your options, the better prepared you will be to put your language skills to good use as you earn a living in future.

Books

Career Ideas for Kids Who Like Talking (Career Ideas for Kids), Diane Lindsey Reeves, Checkmark Books, 2007

Easy Peasy Chinese: Mandarin Chinese for Beginners (Book & CD), Dorling Kindersley, 2007

First 1000 Words in Arabic (Usborne First 1000 Words), Heather Amery and Stephen Cartwright, Usborne, 2001

Way-Cool French Phrase Book: The French that Kids Really Speak, Jane Wightwick, McGraw-Hill, 2013

Websites

www.actfl.org/careers-using-language-skills
There are links from this web page to different pdf articles that introduce ways of using languages in travel, tourism and hospitality, healthcare, national security, international development and business careers.

http://europa.eu/kids-corner/index_en.htm
Find out more about the European Union by visiting this website. You can also play games in a variety of languages.

http://ec.europa.eu/unitedkingdom/pdf/languages_take_you_further.pdf
Compare and contrast the languages of Europe, using simple phrases and numbers. You can download a print copy and also try an online audio version!

www.languageswork.org.uk/career_choices.aspx
This website has a great deal of information about careers that use language skills, case studies of people in careers and practical tips on finding jobs.

Index

advertising 27, 30
aid 8, 19, 21, 22, 23, 30
aid workers 22, 23
A-levels 12, 25
allies 8, 30
Arabic 7, 31

bilingual 12, 13
Brazil 5
BTECs 17

campaigns 26, 27, 30
Chinese 7, 31
colleges 11, 27, 31
companies 5, 8, 13, 15,
    26, 30
culture 4, 7, 9, 11, 17,
    21, 27, 28, 30
current affairs 18, 30

databases 13
debates 9
diplomatic service officers
    14, 15
disasters 22, 23, 29, 30
DVDs 7

embassies 14, 15
emergency response
    programmes 22
European Commission
    Traineeship Schemes 19
European Parliament 9, 19

European Union (EU) 5, 18,
    30, 31
European Union officials 18,
    19

flight attendants 20, 21
Foreign and Commonwealth
    Office (FCO) 14, 15
foreign correspondents 28,
    29
freelancers 7, 11, 30
French 7, 31

GCSEs 17, 21
German 5, 7
governments 8, 15, 22, 30
grammar 5, 9, 30

immigrants 24, 25, 30
immigration officers 24, 25
international relations 4, 30
internships 23, 30
interpreters 8, 9, 12, 13

journalists 9, 27, 28

language teachers 10, 11

marketing 26, 27, 30
marketing campaign
    managers 26, 27
multicultural 4, 30
multilingual 12, 30

natural disasters 22, 23
    29, 30
non-governmental
    organisations (NGOs) 23

officials 14, 19, 22

parliamentary committees
passports 16, 24, 25
PGCEs 11
politicians 8
portfolios 27, 30
publishers 6, 7

representatives 16, 17
Russia 5, 14
Russians 7

Save the Children 23
secretaries 12, 13
social networks 27, 30
Spanish 7, 13

tourism 5, 16, 17, 31
translators 6, 7, 13

United Nations (UN) 12, 3
universities 11

video games 7

wars 4